Millicent E. Selsam

Tree Flowers

illustrated by Carol Lerner

William Morrow and Company
New York   1984

To Katie and Margaret

M.E.S.

For Connie Epstein

C.L.

The author and the illustrator wish to thank Dr. Thomas S. Elias, Assistant Director, Cary Arboretum of the New York Botanical Garden, Millbrook, New York, for checking the text and illustrations of this book.

We would also like to thank Dr. George Ware, Dendrologist of the Morton Arboretum in Lisle, Illinois, for supplying some of the more elusive flowering specimens.

Library of Congress Cataloging in Publication Data
Selsam, Millicent Ellis, 1912- Tree flowers.
Summary: Text and drawings follow the growth cycle of twelve common flowering trees: Pussy willow, white oak, sugar maple, elm, apple, horse chestnut, flowering dogwood, magnolia, witch hazel, black walnut, black locust, and tulip tree.
1. Trees—Juvenile literature. 2. Angiosperms—Juvenile literature. 3. Flowering trees—Juvenile literature. [1. Flowering trees. 2. Trees] I. Lerner, Carol, ill. II. Title. QK475.8.S43 1984 582.16 83-17353
ISBN 0-688-02768-7
ISBN 0-688-02769-5 (lib. bdg.)

Book design by Cindy Simon

Contents

Introduction

If YOU ASK PEOPLE TO NAME A FEW TREE FLOWERS, THEY WILL probably say magnolia or dogwood or apple, because these flowers are easily noticed. They also remain on the tree for a week or two, so that they are likely to be seen. But few people know tree flowers such as willow, elm, maple, or walnut. These flowers are tiny, hard to reach, often have no petals, and last only a few days.

Tree flowers are beautiful to look at, but they serve an important function for the tree as well. Trees, like most other plants, reproduce by making seeds, which can then grow into new trees. The seed-producing parts are in the center of the flower.

The male part of the flower is called the *stamen*. It has a little bag at the top called an *anther*. Inside are *pollen grains*. When the pollen is ripe, the anther bursts and releases it.

The female part of the flower is the *pistil*. The top of it, called the *stigma*, has a sticky or a hairy surface that traps pollen grains. The middle part is the *style*. It connects the stigma and the *ovary*, which is at the base of the pistil. Inside the ovary are *ovules*, or seeds-to-be. They will become seeds only if they are *fertilized*, or joined, by the contents of a pollen grain.

In some types of plants and trees, the flowers do not have both stamens and pistils. Each flower may have only male or only female parts. This is true of pussy willow and oak flowers. The male and female flowers may grow on the same tree or on separate ones. In either case, the pollen from the male flowers must reach the female flowers.

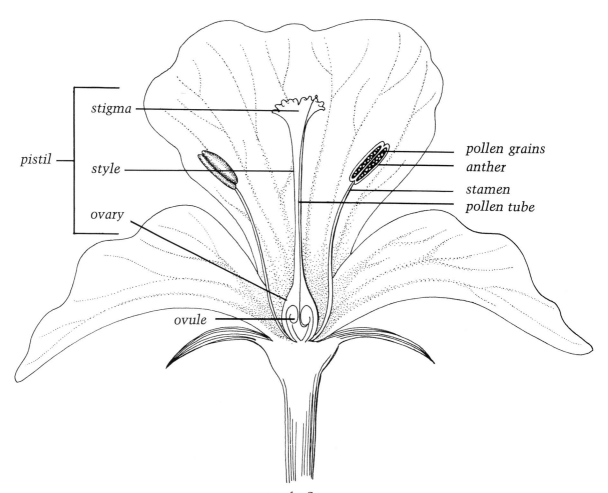

pistil
stigma
style
ovary

pollen grains
anther
stamen
pollen tube

ovule

parts of a flower

The male flowers of many flowering trees grow in long clusters, called *catkins*. Their stamens are usually long and dangle down, open to the wind. When a breeze shakes the catkins, clouds of pollen float away. Most of the pollen is wasted. Some may carpet a pond with yellow dust. Some may land on the roof of a building or even in a cow's ear. Some may reach the female flowers of a different kind of tree. But some pollen grains do reach the hairy stigmas of the same type of flowers.

The female flower of a wind-pollinated tree, such as the oak, is usually tiny and has no petals. The pollen carried by the wind can easily reach the stigmas. A tree flower that is pollinated by insects, however, is very different. Usually it has colorful petals, like an apple blossom, which are visible from a long distance away. As bees and other insects enter the flowers to get *nectar*, the sweet juice produced by the flowers, they are covered with grains of pollen. When they fly to other flowers, the pollen is rubbed off onto the sticky stigmas. Once the pollen reaches the stigma this way, the flower has been *cross-pollinated*.

Some flowers may pollinate themselves—that is, the pollen falls on the stigma of the same flower. This is called *self-pollination*.

When the pollen lands on the stigma, each grain sends out a tube that grows down through the style to the ovules in the ovary. A *sperm cell* inside the pollen tube unites with an *egg cell* inside an ovule. Once the egg cell is joined with the sperm, the ovules change into *seeds*. The ovary around them changes, too. It grows bigger as the seeds develop and becomes a *fruit*. A fruit is any part of the plant that has seeds in it.

Sometimes the ovary becomes a fleshy fruit like an apple. Sometimes it becomes a dry capsule, a pod, or a nut. But all fruits must at some point free their seeds so they can be carried by the wind or insects or animals, such as birds and squirrels, to places where they can grow into new trees.

In this book, we will look at a dozen trees, selected to give samples of various types of flowers. The text is meant to introduce and to excite interest in the world of tree flowers, so detailed technical descriptions of the flowers and their growth cycles are kept to a minimum. The illustrations, though, do show the structure and development of each flower. A life-size scale has been maintained wherever possible. However, most of the individual tiny flowers are shown enlarged. The parts of some specimens are shown reduced: the leaves, fruits, and flowers of the horse chestnut; the flowers and leaves of the magnolia; and the fruits and leaves of oak and maple. Many of the illustrations show the flowers with petals removed so that the essential reproductive organs can be clearly seen.

fertilized pistils
after stamens and petals
have dropped

developing
fruits

mature fruits
(follicles)

seed

Southern Magnolia

Magnolia grandiflora

THE BUDS OF THE SOUTHERN MAGNOLIA TREE OPEN INTO large creamy white flowers from late spring to midsummer. They are big enough to be seen from a distance of a mile, and their sweet smell fills the air all around them.

In the center of each flower is a column of pistils joined together. They are surrounded at the bottom by many golden-colored stamens.

After pollination and fertilization, the stamens and petals drop off and the pistils develop into a cluster of conelike fruits, each called a *follicle*. Each follicle splits open, and two fleshy red seeds slip out. They hang on slender white threads for a week or two before falling to the ground. While they dangle, they are an invitation to birds.

The buds of the Southern magnolia tree have been used by the Chinese as medicine and also to season rice.

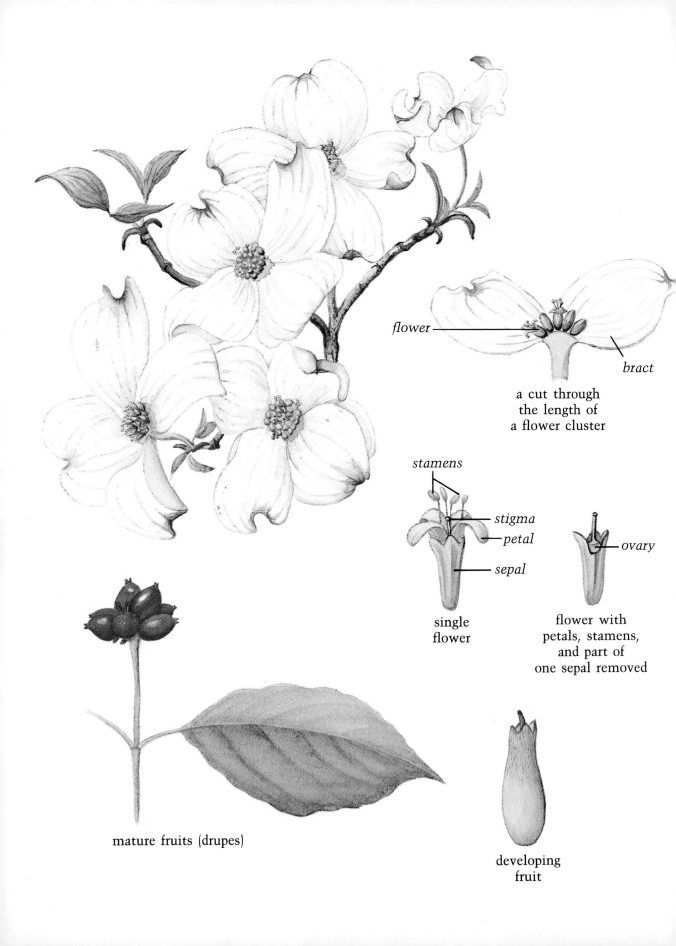

flower

bract

a cut through
the length of
a flower cluster

stamens

stigma

petal

sepal

single
flower

ovary

flower with
petals, stamens,
and part of
one sepal removed

mature fruits (drupes)

developing
fruit

Flowering Dogwood

Cornus florida

In the spring, if you see a tree that seems to be holding layer upon layer of white or pink flowers, it is probably a dogwood tree. But when you look closer at one of the flowers, you will find that it is not a flower at all. What appears to be four red-tipped white petals are really a kind of leaf, called a *bract*. The tiny true flowers are clustered together in the center.

Each little true flower has four curled-back petals, four *sepals* (leaflike parts just outside the petals), four stamens, and a tiny green pistil in the center.

Once it is pollinated and fertilized, the ovary at the base of the pistil ripens into a bright red, egg-shaped fruit called a *drupe*. In the fall, it becomes pulpy and juicy, and a squirrel or bird eats it for food. The seed inside the fruit passes through the animal's body and drops to the ground. This is how dogwood seeds are scattered to new places where the trees can grow.

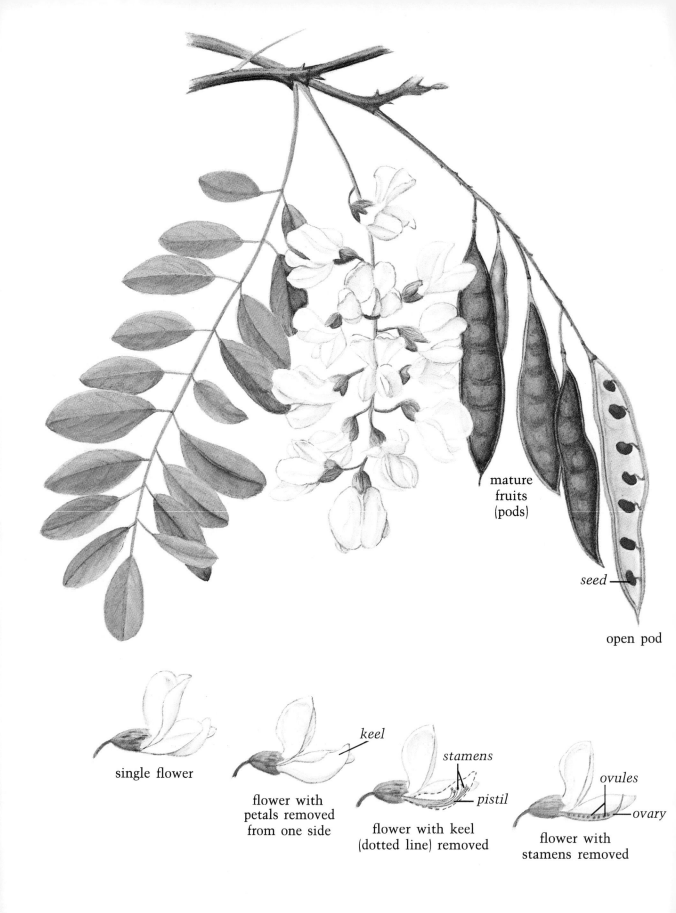

mature
fruits
(pods)

seed —

open pod

single flower

flower with
petals removed
from one side

keel

flower with keel
(dotted line) removed

stamens

pistil

ovules

ovary

flower with
stamens removed

Black Locust

Robinia pseudoacacia

WHEN A WIND BLOWS ACROSS A BLACK LOCUST TREE IN flower, you might see some sweet-smelling white flowers fall to the ground. While still on the tree the flowers hang in drooping clusters.

Each flower looks like a sweet pea. Two of the petals are joined together into something that looks like the keel of a boat. When this *keel* is removed or the petals fall, you can see a tiny ovary in the center of each flower. After pollination and fertilization, each ovary ripens into a brown pod two to four inches long. The pod resembles a green pea pod and contains four to eight brown seeds that look like beans. The pods hang on the tree until winter. Then they open, allowing the seeds to drop out. Sometimes the whole pod, with its seeds intact, is carried by the wind to a new growing area.

Early Americans used the tough wood of the black locust to make spoons, platters, and furniture. They also used it for fence posts, building material, and railroad ties.

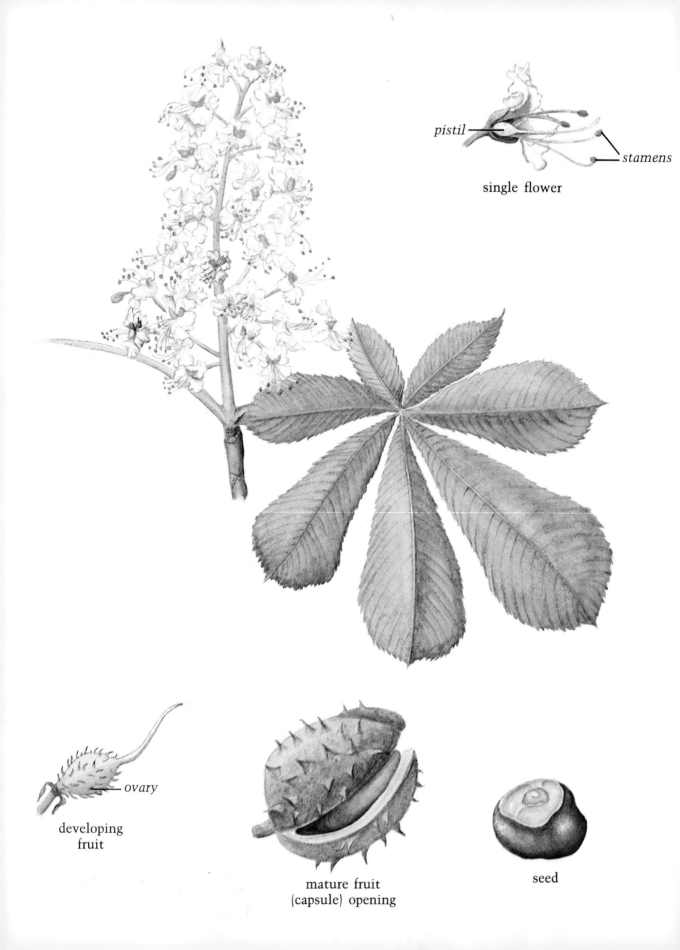

pistil

stamens

single flower

ovary

developing
fruit

mature fruit
(capsule) opening

seed

Horse Chestnut

Aesculus hippocastanum

A TREE THAT LOOKS AS THOUGH IT IS BEARING THICK WHITE candles is probably a horse chestnut tree. In May, tall white clusters of flowers unfold, hundreds at a time. That is when bees and wasps will gather to suck the nectar at the bottom of the flowers.

Each flower has five white petals spotted with yellow and red. Long yellow stamens protrude far out of the flowers. This tree may bear some flowers without pistils, in which case they will not give rise to seeds.

The petals fall after the flowers have been pollinated and fertilized. The ovaries change into green prickly fruits, called *capsules*. In October the green husks break open into three parts and reveal the round, shiny nuts in the center. They are bitter and poisonous. Now these nuts can fall to the ground and grow into new trees.

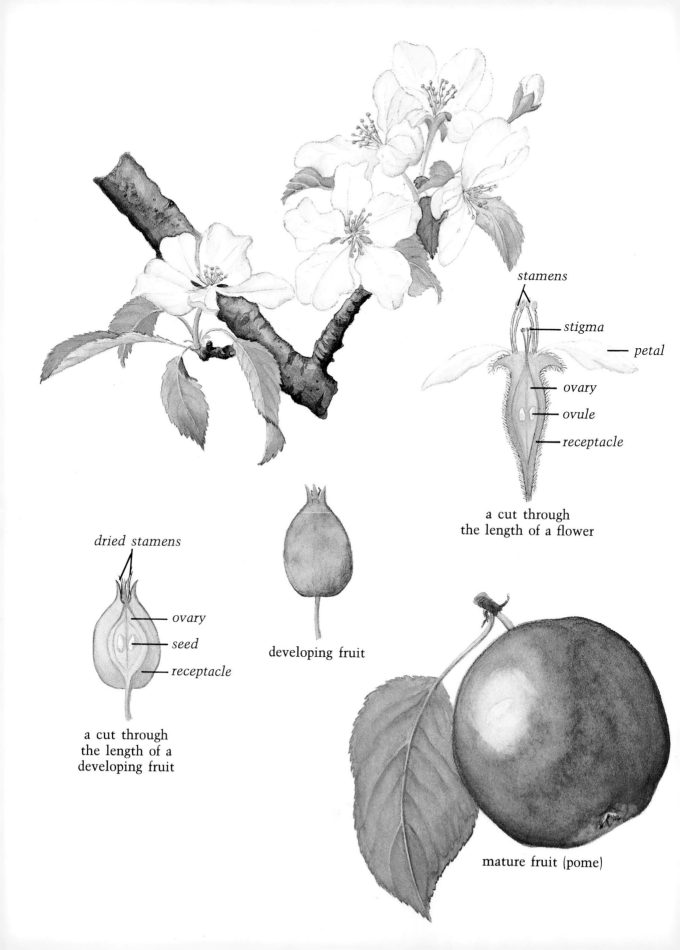

stamens

stigma

petal

ovary

ovule

receptacle

a cut through
the length of a flower

dried stamens

ovary

seed

receptacle

a cut through
the length of a
developing fruit

developing fruit

mature fruit (pome)

Apple

Malus pumila

IN THE SPRINGTIME, YOU WILL PROBABLY SEE APPLE TREES
covered with sweet-smelling, light pink blossoms. They are borne
on short, stubby twigs.

Each flower contains many pale green stamens and five pistils.
The pistils are joined at the base, forming a five-lobed ovary. A
cuplike swollen flower stalk called a *receptacle* surrounds it.

Apple flowers are sweet. Bees and other insects come to suck
the nectar produced by the flower and to gather pollen. In doing
so they unknowingly carry pollen grains from one flower to
another and pollinate them.

There are five chambers in the ovary and in each chamber there
are ovules. If the ovules are fertilized, the ovary and receptacle
swell into a juicy apple. If all the ovules are fertilized, you will get
a fully rounded apple. If some ovules are not fertilized, the tissues
around them do not swell and this results in a lopsided fruit.

The fruit of the apple tree is known as a *pome*. As we know, it
is very good to eat. In addition, applewood is used for making
bowls and is also good firewood.

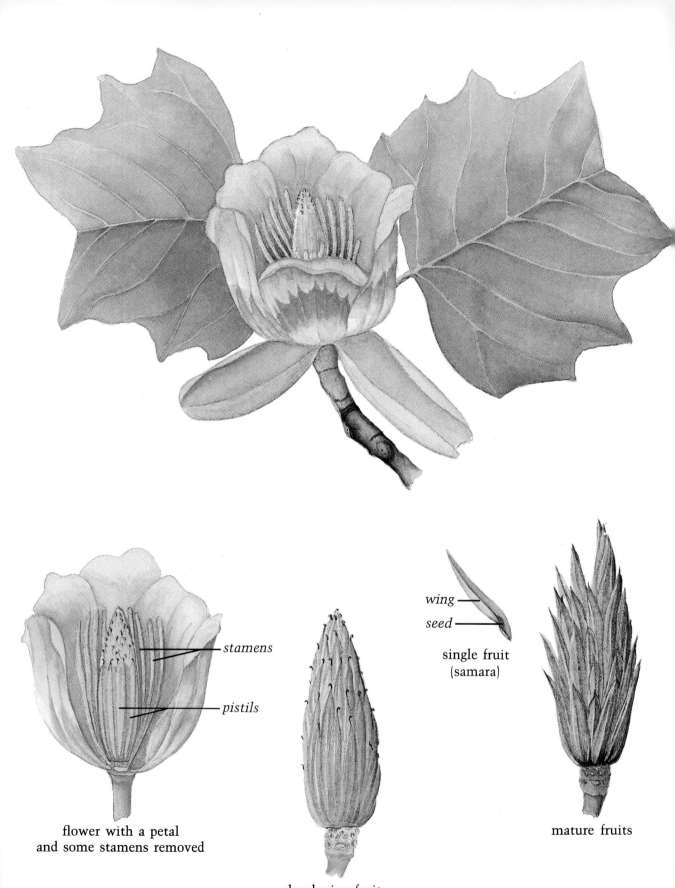

stamens

pistils

flower with a petal
and some stamens removed

developing fruits

wing

seed

single fruit
(samara)

mature fruits

Tulip Tree

Liriodendron tulipifera

THE TULIP TREE GETS ITS NAME FROM ITS FLOWERS, WHICH look like tulips. Late in May or in early June, these large flowers open to reveal orange petals tipped with pale green. The petals surround the numerous golden stamens. The stamens, in turn, surround the pistils, which cling together around a central axis.

If pollination and fertilization take place, this central group of pistils ripens into a pale brown, cone-shaped cluster of dry fruits, called *samaras*, each with a winged seed. In the winter, the cone, from the top down, breaks up into the winged seeds. The seeds are eaten and spread by squirrels and birds who drop them while feeding. They also pass through the animals bodies after being eaten and drop to the ground that way. Tulip tree seeds also float on streams and brooks near the parent tree and are carried to new growing areas.

In Annapolis, Maryland, there is a giant tulip tree under which the colonists and Indians made a treaty of peace in 1652. After the American Revolution, people gathered under that same tree to celebrate peace. That is why the tulip tree is sometimes called the "liberty" tree.

19

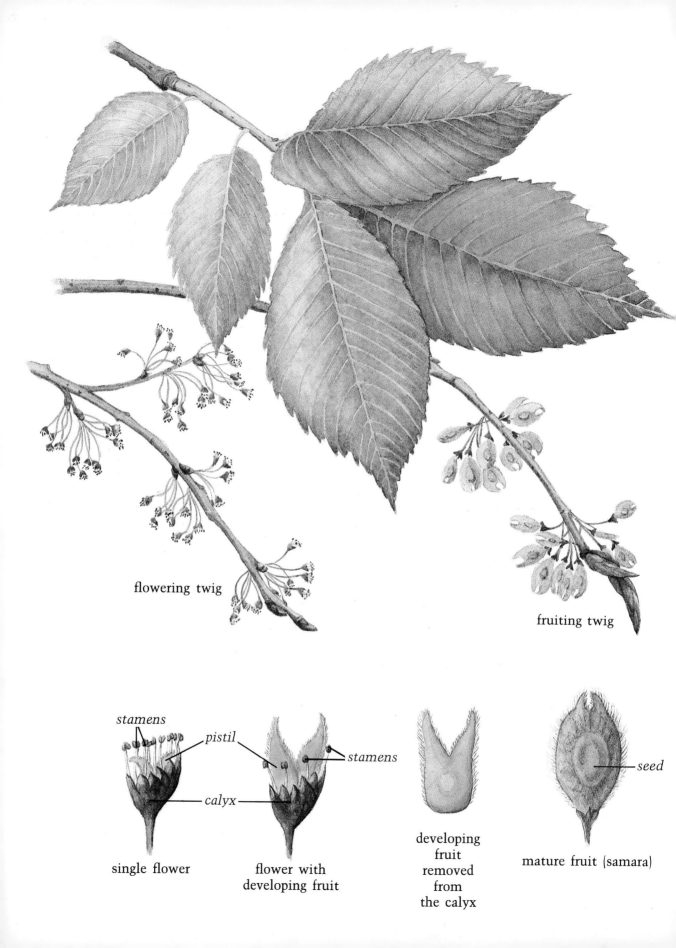

flowering twig

fruiting twig

stamens

pistil

stamens

calyx

seed

single flower

flower with developing fruit

developing fruit removed from the calyx

mature fruit (samara)

American Elm

Ulmus americana

THE ELMS BURST INTO BLOOM IN EARLY SPRING, BUT THE flowers are so tiny that all you can see of them is a haze of purple in the treetops.

Many years ago, elm trees were favorite places for Indian tribes to gather. In the spring, one Indian would say to another, "Meet me when the elms are in flower." Since the flowers only last a few days, no one would have to wait too long for a friend to appear.

Elm flowers grow on long drooping stems. They have no petals, but they do have an outside covering called a *calyx*. When ripe, seven to nine red anthers on each flower open and give off puffs of white pollen. The stigmas of the pistils are hairy and easily trap some of the millions of pollen grains carried by the wind.

Once the flowers have been pollinated and fertilized the ovaries change into papery winged fruits, the samaras. Thousands of these fruits drop to the ground when the wind blows. Most of the seeds inside the fruits die unless they fall on moist soil. Those that do fall on moist soil sprout in a day or two.

American elm trees were once the pride of New England. However, in the 1930s they were infected by the Dutch elm disease, which is caused by a fungus carried from tree to tree by bark beetles. Many trees were lost in this way. So far spraying with insecticides has helped somewhat but not enough. The American elms are still in danger.

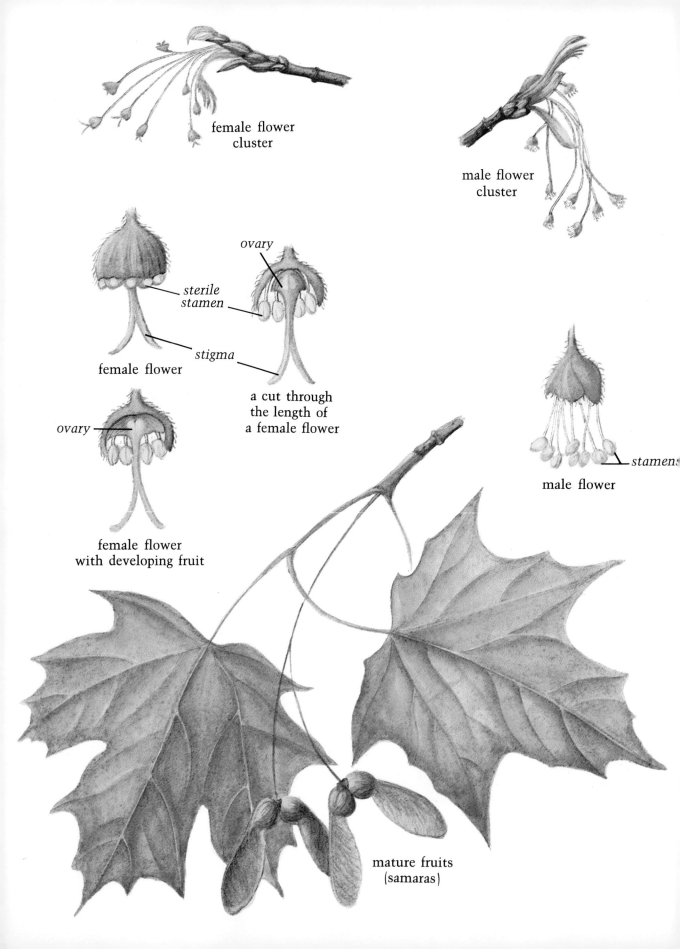

female flower
cluster

male flower
cluster

ovary

*sterile
stamen*

ovary

stigma

female flower

a cut through
the length of
a female flower

ovary

male flower

stamens

female flower
with developing fruit

mature fruits
(samaras)

Sugar Maple

Acer saccharum

THE YELLOW DROOPING CLUSTERS OF THE SUGAR MAPLE flowers appear together with the leaves and give the whole tree a yellow haze. Each cluster bears male or female flowers.

The male flower holds seven or eight long drooping stamens. The female flower has a pistil as well as stamens, but these stamens are small and do not produce pollen. They are sterile. Male and female flowers can grow on the same tree, but they are always in separate clusters.

After pollination and fertilization, the ovules slowly change into seeds. Around them the ovaries swell and develop thin wings. The mature winged maple fruits are the samaras. In the autumn when the wind blows, they spin away from the parent tree like little helicopters.

The wood of the sugar maple is much used for furniture, and its sap gives us our familiar maple syrup.

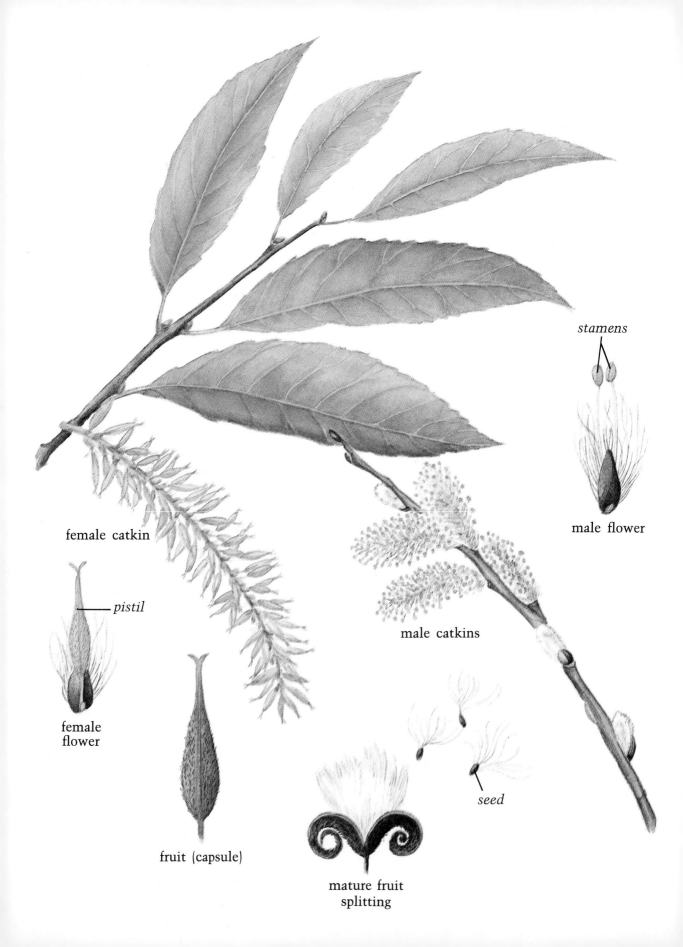

stamens

male flower

female catkin

pistil

female
flower

fruit (capsule)

male catkins

seed

mature fruit
splitting

Pussy Willow

Salix discolor

IN THE WINTER, YOU CAN SEE THE REDDISH BROWN BUDS ON THE pussy willows. In early spring, the buds open into soft gray "pussies." The pussies then open into catkins. If you put pussy willow twigs into water, you can see them opening for yourself.

You may see two different types of catkins. One kind bears the male flowers, each with two stamens. The yellow pollen in the anthers of these stamens give the whole catkin a yellow color. The other kind of catkin is green and bears tiny bottle-shaped female flowers, each with one pistil. Male and female flowers are borne on different trees.

The wind may carry pollen to the female flowers, but insects also seek the flowers' nectar and pollinate the flowers by flying to and from male and female flowers carrying loads of pollen.

Once pollination and fertilization take place, the ovary of the pistil changes into a bottle-shaped fruit called a *capsule*. In early summer, the capsule splits open and the seeds pop out. They have silky hairs that act like parachutes and help to carry them through the air. The seeds must soon find moist places in which to sprout. Otherwise they die.

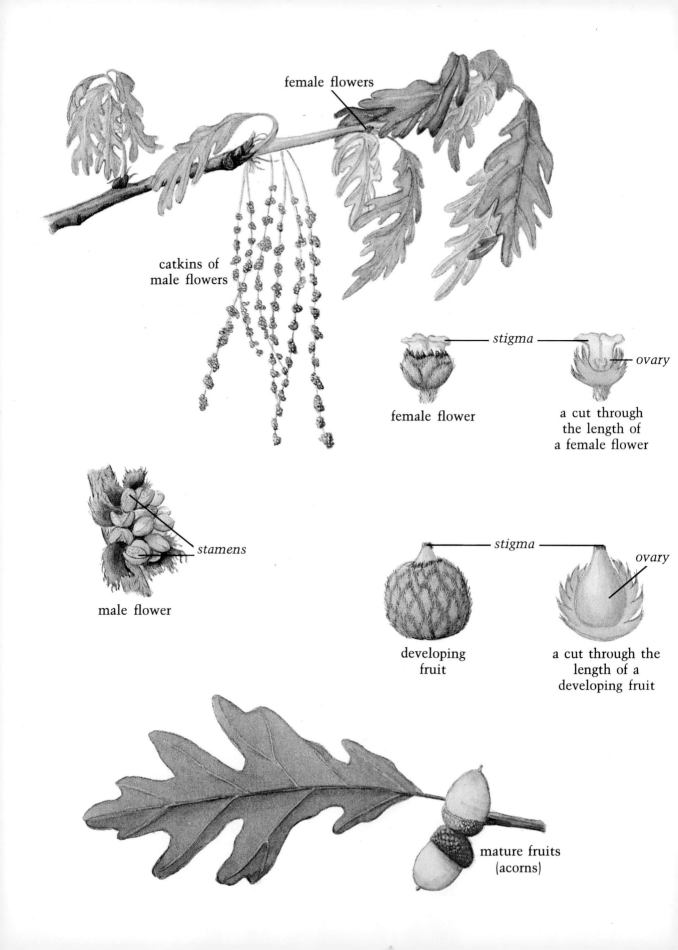

female flowers

catkins of
male flowers

stigma

ovary

female flower

a cut through
the length of
a female flower

stamens

male flower

stigma

ovary

developing
fruit

a cut through the
length of a
developing fruit

mature fruits
(acorns)

White Oak

Quercus alba

As the young leaves are unfolding in the springtime, long tassels of male flowers hang from the branches of the oak tree. They are easy to see, but the female flowers are hard to find. They are tucked away at the point where the leaves grow out of the twigs. The male flowers greatly outnumber the female flowers and produce clouds of pollen that are carried by the wind and eventually reach the stigmas of the female flowers.

After the flower has been pollinated and fertilized, the ovaries rapidly change into the fruits we call *acorns*. By autumn they are mature and soon after they fall can sprout into new white oak trees. If they lie on the ground uncovered, they may freeze, but squirrels bury acorns in the ground as a winter food supply. Since they do not always find all the acorns they bury, many remain buried, and the seed inside grows into a new tree.

The meat of the acorn is sweet and edible. Early settlers and American Indians boiled them or ground them into meal. The wood of the oak is used for boats, railroad ties, floors, and furniture.

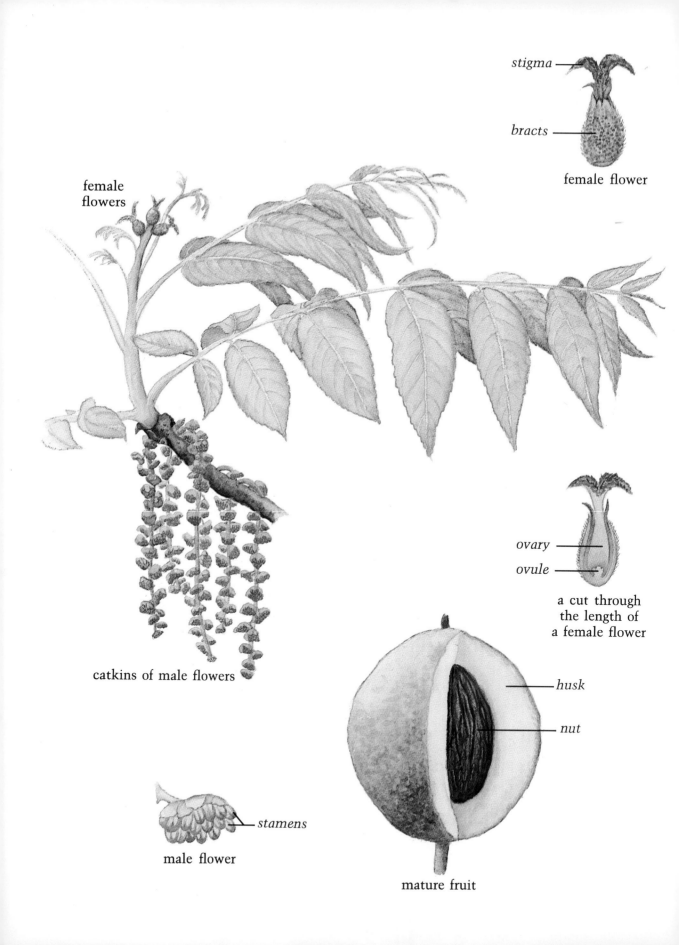

stigma

bracts

female flower

female
flowers

catkins of male flowers

ovary

ovule

a cut through
the length of
a female flower

husk

nut

stamens

male flower

mature fruit

Black Walnut

Juglans nigra

THE BLACK WALNUT TREE HAS TWO KINDS OF FLOWERS, MALE and female. The male flowers hang down in long catkins. Many stamens in each flower produce masses of pollen, which is carried by the wind to the female flowers. Female flowers are tiny and difficult to locate on the tree. Their pistils are shaped like little vases and are covered with bracts, a kind of leaf. Big feathery stigmas at the top of the pistil catch the pollen as it floats through the air.

After pollination and fertilization, the ovary of the pistil changes into a ball-shaped green fruit. In the center of the fruit there is a seed called a *nut*. It has a hard bony shell. Around it is a thick fleshy husk.

The entire fruit—nut, husk, and all—falls to the ground in October. There the husk shrivels up and releases the nut. It is sweet and edible, but the shell is so thick and tough that it is hard to crack. However, squirrels and bluejays manage to crack the nuts open. Many nuts are buried in the ground by squirrels as a winter supply of food. If they are not found again they will sprout in the spring into new black walnut trees.

The wood of the black walnut tree is used for furniture and carpentry work of all kinds.

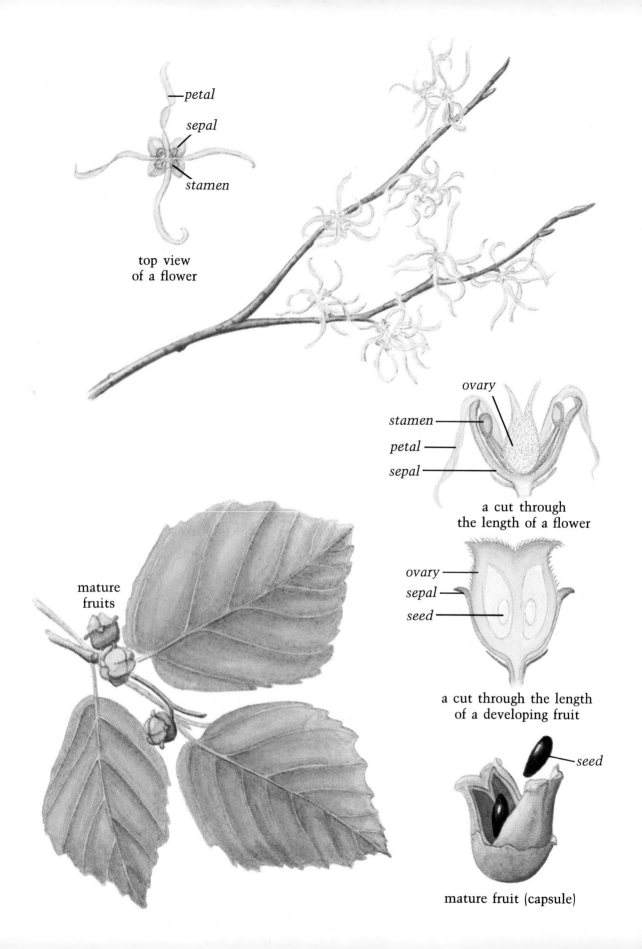

petal

sepal

stamen

top view
of a flower

mature
fruits

ovary

stamen

petal

sepal

a cut through
the length of a flower

ovary

sepal

seed

a cut through the length
of a developing fruit

seed

mature fruit (capsule)

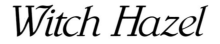

Witch Hazel

Hamamelis virginiana

IN AUTUMN, WHEN MOST OF THE LEAVES HAVE FALLEN FROM THE trees, the pale yellow, ribbonlike flowers of witch hazel appear. Four long petals stand out above four *sepals*, which are the parts just outside the petals.

Once the flower is pollinated and fertilized, the ovary of the flower slowly develops into a woody fruit called a capsule. When fully ripe the following fall, the capsule opens with a bang and ejects two shiny black seeds. If you keep a branch of witch hazel in your house, you will hear loud snaps as the seeds fly across the room.

In the early days of the United States, people believed that the forked branches of witch hazel could locate gold or water by dipping down toward the earth by itself wherever these substances lay beneath the surface. The witch hazel has no such magical properties, but some people still believe these old superstitions.

The name witch hazel comes from this folklore about the branches being able to locate water and minerals. It has other names, too—winter bloom, from its late-appearing flowers, and snapping alder, from the way the seeds shoot out of the capsules.

An extract of witch hazel bark, twigs, and leaves is used as a soothing lotion for cuts and bruises.

THE TWELVE TREE FLOWERS IN THIS BOOK ARE JUST SAMPLES OF the many kinds that exist. Most bloom in early spring. When they come out, look at them closely. Watch the buds open and the flowers grow. See how they change as the days go by, and how the fruits and seeds form. Enjoy the wonder of tree flowers.

DATE DUE
